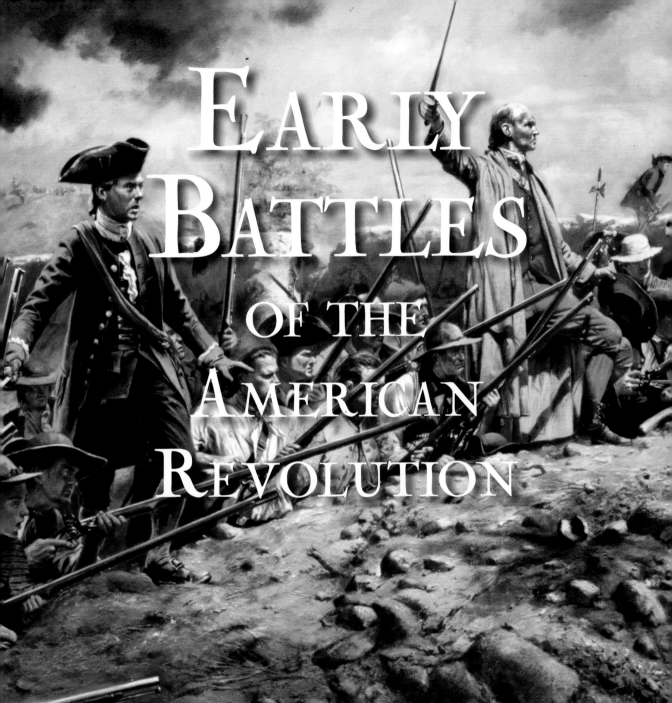

EARLY BATTLES
OF THE
AMERICAN
REVOLUTION

BY JOHN HAMILTON

VISIT US AT
WWW.ABDOPUBLISHING.COM

Published by ABDO Publishing Company, PO Box 398166, Minneapolis, MN 55439.
Copyright ©2013 by Abdo Consulting Group, Inc. International copyrights reserved in all
countries. No part of this book may be reproduced in any form without written permission from
the publisher. ABDO & Daughters™ is a trademark and logo of ABDO Publishing Company.

Printed in the United States of America, North Mankato, Minnesota.
112012
012013

 PRINTED ON RECYCLED PAPER

Editor: Sue Hamilton
Graphic Design: John Hamilton
Cover Design: Neil Klinepier
Cover: Painting by Don Troiani, www.historicalartprints.com
Interior Photos and Illustrations: AP Images, p. 6, 7, 21, 28; Corbis, p. 26; Getty Images, p. 5,
8-9, 10, 11, 14-15, 19, 23; John Hamilton, p. 7, 10, 11, 12-13, 16, 18, 20, 24, 27; Military and
Historical Image Bank, p. 1, 17, 25, 29; National Archives, p. 22; Thinkstock, p. 3; Yale Center for
British Art, p. 4.

ABDO Booklinks
To learn more about the American Revolution, visit ABDO Publishing Company online. Web
sites about the American Revolution are featured on our Book Links pages. These links are
routinely monitored and updated to provide the most current information available.
Web site: www.abdopublishing.com

Library of Congress Control Number: 2012945991

Cataloging-in-Publication Data

Hamilton, John.
Early battles of the American Revolution / John Hamilton.
    p. cm. — (American Revolution)
Includes index.
ISBN 978-1-61783-679-4
1. United States—History—Revolution, 1775-1783—Campaigns—Juvenile literature. I. Title.
973.3/3—dc22

2012945991

CONTENTS

PREPARING FOR WAR

The American War of Independence erupted on April 19, 1775, at the Battles of Lexington and Concord, just west of Boston, Massachusetts. A modest British mission to seize illegal weapons turned into a disaster as colonial militia rose up against the Redcoats. It was a rude awakening for the British. The rebels fired their muskets from behind trees and stone fences, then melted away into the woods. The British were caught off guard by this nontraditional style of warfare. They were trained to fight in large groups on an open battlefield. They took heavy losses, with 73 dead and 200 wounded or missing.

British leaders, including General Thomas Gage, were caught flat-footed. How was it possible that the world's most powerful army had been beaten by an ill-trained colonial militia, most of them common laborers and farmers? The British realized they had greatly underestimated the colonists's will to fight for freedom.

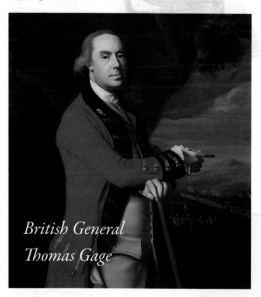

British General Thomas Gage

*Reenactors portraying British
Redcoats firing on colonial militia*

British troops retreating under fire from colonial militia after the Battles of Concord and Lexington.

By nightfall, the British troops had retreated to the safety of Boston. They were pinned against the sea, with a garrison of only about 4,000 men. In the darkness, General Gage could see the campfires of thousands of rebel troops on the hills surrounding the city. His situation that night seemed grim.

Within days Boston was surrounded by 7,000 colonial militia troops. Many of them were encamped in nearby Cambridge, Massachusetts, under the command of militia leader General Artemas Ward. As they fortified their positions, their spirits soared. They had proven that the British Army could be beaten.

Under British occupation, more than half the citizens of Boston fled the city, leaving it with a civilian population of about 7,000. Many were loyalists who sided with the British. Food shortages and lack of supplies made life difficult. And there was always the feeling that at any moment American artillery would soon bombard the city.

When news of the Battles of Lexington and Concord reached Great Britain, King George III and Parliament were shocked. But they

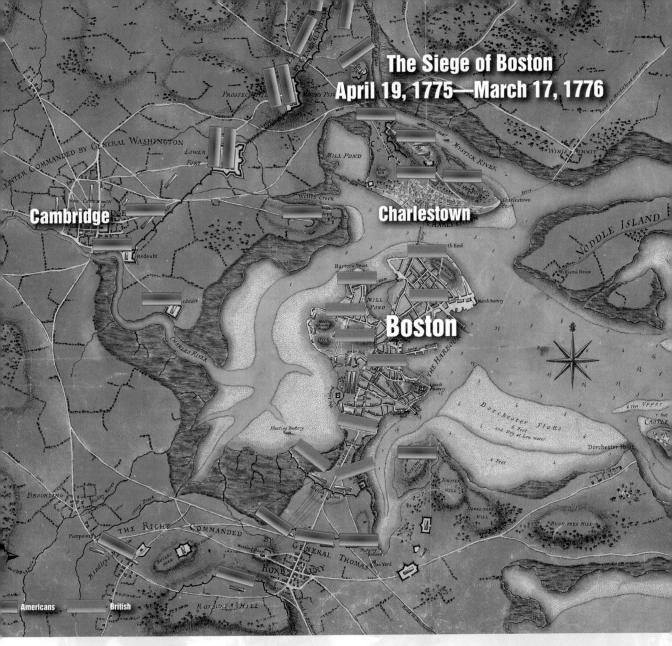

Cambridge

Charlestown

Boston

Americans   British

did not believe the colonists could win a long war against the most powerful army on Earth. "I am of the opinion," the king wrote, "that when once these rebels have felt a smart blow, they will submit."

Even though the British were under siege, the Royal Navy had complete control of Boston Harbor. General Gage waited as supplies and reinforcements began streaming in. He couldn't launch a full assault yet, but he knew it was only a matter of time. He waited, eager to break out of the city and crush the American rebellion.

May 10, 1775

THE SECOND CONTINENTAL CONGRESS

For the second time in less than a year, representatives of the colonies met to discuss the violent conflict with Great Britain. The Second Continental Congress gathered in Philadelphia, Pennsylvania, on May 10, 1775.

Members of the Congress included some of the most brilliant politicians and statesmen of the time. Many of these men are today called the Founding Fathers of the United States. Among the delegates were George Washington and Thomas Jefferson from Virginia, John Adams and John Hancock from Massachusetts, and Benjamin Franklin from Pennsylvania.

Even though the Congress hoped to find a way to make peace, their main job was to plan for war. In fact, the war had already started a month earlier in Boston. A ragtag collection of Massachusetts militias were fighting the British, and doing so with little control or guidance.

The Continental Congress had to take control of the war effort. This would make it much easier to send troops and supplies where they were needed most. A central decision-making government might also give the Patriot cause approval in the eyes of the world. Perhaps the colonies could find allies in their fight against Great Britain.

A statue of George Washington in front of Independence Hall, Philadelphia, Pennsylvania.

As with any group of politicians, there were disagreements about the best course of action to take against Great Britain. But urgency was in the air. The Continental Congress had to agree on a plan, and do it quickly. The fate of a new nation hung in the balance.

May 10, 1775

THE CAPTURE OF FORT TICONDEROGA

On the very day that the Second Continental Congress first met in Philadelphia, Pennsylvania, colonial forces attacked the key British stronghold of Fort Ticonderoga, in the frontier wilderness area of northeastern colonial New York.

The stone walls of Fort Ticonderoga were constructed on high ground overlooking Lake Champlain and Lake George. The area connected the Hudson River Valley with waterways leading into British-held Canada. The fort was a formidable obstacle to any military force passing through.

Left: Fort Ticonderoga from above.

In Boston, Massachusetts, the Patriot militia surrounding British forces trapped in the city lacked supplies, especially cannons and gunpowder. "Fort Ti" was in disrepair and lightly manned. Its artillery and weapons would be a fine prize.

Colonel Ethan Allen commanded a group of about 100 militia troops from Vermont, which was not yet a state. The troops were called the Green Mountain Boys. They were joined by Captain

Above: Ethan Allen, sword in hand, demands that Captain William De La Place surrender Fort Ticonderoga.

Benedict Arnold from Connecticut, who co-commanded the mission.

Before dawn on May 10, 1775, the Americans snuck up to the fort. They found an unlocked door and streamed in. After a brief fight with just 85 defenders, the fort's commander, Captain William De La Place, surrendered. The 70 artillery pieces captured from Fort Ticonderoga would later be very important in the struggle to free Boston from British control.

Left: A cannon at Fort Ticonderoga overlooking the southern narrows of Lake Champlain.

The Continental Army

On June 14, 1775, the Second Continental Congress officially created an army. John Adams at first wanted to adopt the Massachusetts militia. The Congress decided instead to use militia from all 13 colonies. Local militias were still used to battle the British, but the new Continental Army became a true national fighting force.

The next day, on June 15, George Washington of Virginia was chosen to lead the Continental Army. Washington had valuable experience commanding troops in the French and Indian War. He was courageous on the battlefield, and well connected politically. By the end of 1775, he commanded about 27,500 combined militia and Continental troops, an impressive feat considering there was no national army less than a year earlier.

Members of the Continental Army were paid volunteers. They enlisted for a set amount of time, usually one to three years. These citizen-soldiers often brought their own muskets and other weapons. At first, most even wore their own clothes instead of uniforms. They had little training, and needed practice in following orders and handling muskets. But the Patriots had a big advantage: they were fighting for a cause, a chance to create their own republic. With time and training, the Continental Army troops became more disciplined, and earned the grudging respect of British soldiers for their bravery and grit.

Reenactors portraying a regiment of Continental Army troops.

THE SIEGE OF BOSTON

British soldiers clash with colonial militia at the top of Breed's Hill on June 17, 1775. This painting by John Trumbull shows the death of the popular American Patriot leader Major-General Dr. Joseph Warren.

In June 1775, British General Thomas Gage prepared to strike against rebel forces besieging Boston, Massachusetts. For two months British ships had brought reinforcements and supplies. Generals William Howe, Henry Clinton, and John Burgoyne also arrived to help crush the rebellion.

Massachusetts militia forces, led by General Artemas Ward, knew that the hills surrounding Boston were key to keeping the British bottled up. These hills overlooked the city and the harbor. Cannons placed on the high ground would threaten British warships and troops.

On the night of June 16, the Americans dug fortifications, called redoubts, on the Charlestown peninsula, which overlooked Boston to the south. The British response was swift. The following morning, June 17, 1775, thousands of Redcoats rowed across the Charles River and prepared to attack the Patriots.

The famous Battle of Bunker Hill is misnamed. Although the rebels were ordered to occupy Bunker Hill, they had mistakenly set up their strongest redoubts on Breed's Hill, which was less steep and more vulnerable.

All morning British warships bombarded the rebel positions. The weather was hot and oppressive. Finally, that afternoon, the Redcoats marched up Breed's Hill.

Under the command of Colonel William Prescott and General Israel Putnam, the colonial militia fought bravely. Two assaults by British troops were repulsed. A third assault finally broke through the rebel defenses.

Although the British won the battle at Breed's Hill, they failed to break the American siege of Boston. The battle was one of the bloodiest fights of the entire war. The British lost 1,154 killed and wounded, including many officers. The Americans lost 140 killed and 301 wounded. British General Clinton remarked that the battle was "A dear-bought victory; another such would have ruined us."

The British were so angry about the heavy losses that they replaced General Gage with General Howe as commander of British forces in the colonies. They would not launch another major land attack for more than a year.

Spirits soared among the Americans. Two weeks later, on July 3, 1775, George Washington arrived to take command.

The new Continental Army had very little discipline. Washington set out to change that. "Discipline is the soul of an army," he wrote. As the months of siege dragged on, Washington drilled his men in European-style military tactics.

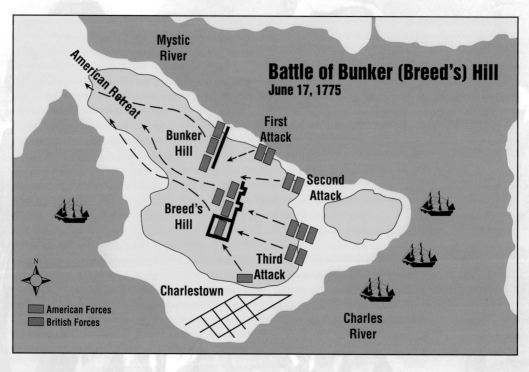

Battle of Bunker (Breed's) Hill
June 17, 1775

Mystic River

American Retreat

First Attack

Bunker Hill

Second Attack

Breed's Hill

Third Attack

Charlestown

American Forces
British Forces

Charles River

N

British troops break through the American redoubt at Breed's Hill.

Washington also worked hard to find food and ammunition, which were always in short supply.

During the winter of 1775-1776, Washington sent Colonel Henry Knox to newly captured Fort Ticonderoga. Knox returned in March, having dragged 50 pieces of artillery across icebound New England. Washington promptly installed the cannons and mortars in position on Dorchester Heights, overlooking Boston to the north.

The Patriot artillery made the British position impossible to defend. On March 17, 1776, General Howe's forces evacuated Boston. They boarded ships and sailed to the safety of Halifax, Nova Scotia.

A triumphant Washington and his rebel army marched into Boston. It was the first major campaign victory of the war. In addition, the captured weapons the British abandoned would be put to good use for the long fight yet to come.

THE INVASION OF CANADA

In the autumn of 1775, an American force of about 1,000 men invaded Canada. Their goal was to capture the towns of Montreal and Québec along the Saint Lawrence River. They hoped to prevent the British Royal Navy from landing an invasion force and attacking New England from the north. The Americans also hoped to convince Canadians to join the rebel effort as a 14th colony.

Led by Generals Philip Schuyler and Richard Montgomery, the Americans struck north from Fort Ticonderoga. They captured a series of forts before overrunning Montreal. Then they turned northeast, toward Québec.

Meanwhile, a second group, commanded by Colonel Benedict Arnold, made its way north through the rugged wilderness of today's Maine. After a grueling march, they finally linked up with Montgomery's troops near Québec.

The death of General Montgomery during the ill-fated American attack of Québec.

By this time, a harsh northern winter had set in. Disease and injuries sidelined many men.

During a blinding snowstorm on December 31, 1775, the Americans launched a surprise assault on Québec. The attack was a disaster. Many Americans were killed, including General Montgomery.

The Americans laid siege to the city, but by the spring of 1776 British reinforcements forced them to retreat south.

Colonel Arnold fought a fierce naval battle in October near Lake Champlain's Valcour Island, but his little fleet of gunboats was destroyed. The British, although victorious, delayed a full-scale invasion of the colonies. Winter was coming. They moved back to Canada, where they wouldn't threaten the colonies again until 1777. The American expedition had been defeated, but it bought valuable time for the young country to train its army and rally support.

EARLY SOUTHERN BATTLES

Despite early battlefield successes, many colonists remained loyal to King George III and Great Britain. These loyalists, also called Tories, did not want independence. Their language and customs were British. Many had successful businesses trading with Great Britain, or had relatives that lived in the mother country. Others were afraid of the powerful British Army. The British military hoped Tories would help them extinguish the rebellion.

In the southern colony of North Carolina, there was a sharp divide between the Patriots and the Tories. In February 1776, about 1,600 Tories gathered and marched toward the coast, hoping to join with their British allies. On February 27, a group of Patriots blocked the Tories at the Battle of Moore's Creek Bridge.

American Forces
British Forces

The Battle of Fort Sullivan
June 28, 1776

N

Fort Sullivan

Sullivan's Island

SC
Charleston

Americans at Fort Sullivan holding off an attack by British warships.

The Tories, many of them from Scotland, passed through a swampy area and encountered a wooden bridge. Unaware of a Patriot ambush awaiting them, the sword-waving Tories marched forward to the shrill wailing of bagpipes. Suddenly, they were cut down by withering fire from Patriot muskets. By the end of the battle, 30 Tories were killed, 40 wounded, and 850 captured. The Patriots lost just two men.

Undeterred by this loss, on June 28, 1776, British General Henry Clinton and 2,500 Redcoats tried to invade Charleston, South Carolina, by sea. Blocking the harbor was Sullivan's Island, where the Patriots had built a crude fort made of palmetto logs. The nine British warships showered the fort with cannon fire, but the spongy logs and sand absorbed the explosions. With Colonel William Moultrie in command, the Patriot artillery counterattack was devastating. So many British warships were damaged by the end of the day that the Royal Navy was forced to call off the invasion.

July 4, 1776

THE DECLARATION OF INDEPENDENCE

Not long after the Battles of Lexington and Concord, the Second Continental Congress on July 8, 1775, sent a letter to Great Britain's King George III. Called the Olive Branch Petition, the request was a last-ditch effort to negotiate the colonies's grievances with Britain and avoid full-scale war. The petition was ignored by the king. Instead, the monarch declared that the colonies were officially in a state of rebellion, and accelerated the British war effort. The Olive Branch Petition's rejection gave John Adams and other Patriots just the ammo they needed to push for a complete break from Great Britain.

By mid-1776, the majority of American colonists desired independence. They had endured years of unfair taxes and regulations and bloody battles on their home soil. Earlier in the year, writer and political activist Thomas Paine published a bestselling 50-page pamphlet called *Common Sense*. Paine wrote that governments should not oppress the very people

The Declaration of Independence.

The Declaration of Independence is presented to the Second Continental Congress.

they serve. He also made the daring suggestion that common people had the right to govern themselves. *Common Sense* influenced many Americans to support the revolution.

In Philadelphia, Pennsylvania, the Second Continental Congress needed an official document stating why the colonies wanted their freedom. This document, or "declaration," would help rally support among the colonies, and also make their struggle justified in the eyes of the world. Congress hoped that another powerful country, such as France, might help the Americans in their fight.

In late June 1776, Congress was presented with a document created by a five-member committee that included Thomas Jefferson, Benjamin Franklin, John Adams, Robert Livingston, and Roger Sherman. The document spelled out the complaints against Great Britain. It also declared that the colonies were now free and independent states.

For several days, Congress debated the document's wording. Finally, on July 4, 1776, all 56 members representing the 13 colonies signed the Declaration of Independence. It was official: the United States of America was born.

THE FIGHT FOR NEW YORK

The British fled Boston, Massachusetts, in March 1776. After retreating to Halifax, Nova Scotia, they gathered reinforcements and refocused their efforts on a new target: New York City, on the southern tip of Manhattan Island. The port city was not as important as Boston and its busy harbor, but it had great potential value. Whoever controlled New York controlled the Hudson River. The Hudson and its connecting waterways, including Lake Champlain, ran north all the way to Canada. By controlling the Hudson, the British could divide the colonies in two and isolate New England, perhaps making Boston an easier target for eventual capture.

In April, shortly after his victory in Boston, General George Washington moved most of his army to New York. He had guessed the British plan to attack the city. Washington had 19,000 troops at his disposal, but defending such a large area stretched his forces thin. Washington set up a series of defensive forts and trenches along Long Island's Brooklyn Heights.

NEW YORK

Hudson River Valley

CONN.

NEW JERSEY

New York City

Long Island

General George Washington oversees his troops during the New York campaign.

The Delaware Regiment of the Continental Army firing their muskets at the Battle of Long Island, New York, August 27, 1776.

At the end of June, the new commander of British forces, General William Howe, sailed with thousands of Redcoats to Staten Island, across the bay from New York City. Howe amassed nearly 40,000 men, including paid German mercenaries called Hessians. The British Royal Navy guarded the southern entrance to New York Harbor, preventing any rebel interference from the sea.

American soldiers of the Continental Army were mostly inexperienced and poorly equipped.

Morale dipped in the face of the impending British attack. On July 9, to boost his men's spirits, Washington had a copy of the Declaration of Independence read aloud to the troops.

On August 22, General Howe's battle preparations were complete. He moved about 20,000 Redcoats across the narrows of New York Bay and landed on Long Island. Just past midnight on August 27, Howe's forces attacked the badly outnumbered Americans. By morning, a flanking maneuver led

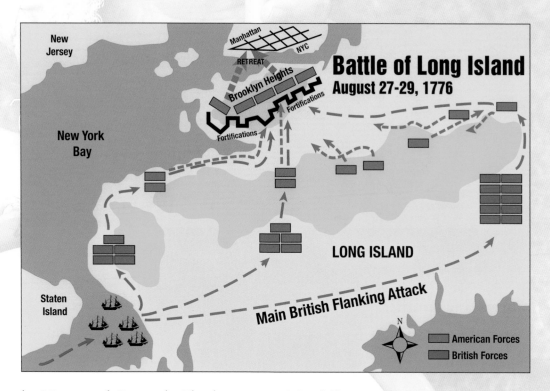

Battle of Long Island
August 27-29, 1776

New Jersey

Manhattan

NYC

RETREAT

Brooklyn Heights

Fortifications

Fortifications

New York Bay

Fortifications

LONG ISLAND

Staten Island

Main British Flanking Attack

N

American Forces
British Forces

by Howe and Generals Charles Cornwallis and Henry Clinton created panic in the American ranks. Hundreds of troops were killed or captured. The Continental Army fell back to its fortifications on Brooklyn Heights. They were surrounded by overwhelming British forces on all sides. Washington was trapped.

Instead of pressing forward and crushing the Americans once and for all, British General Howe halted to reorganize and build defensive positions for his troops.

The following day, terrible weather prevented another British attack. It was just the break General Washington needed. He wasted no time in carrying out a daring plan.

In the early morning darkness of August 29, Washington and his troops began crossing the East River in a flotilla of small boats. By daybreak, his men and most of their equipment were safely on the island of Manhattan. To British General Howe's utter astonishment, Washington and the entire American army had escaped.

The Continental Army escaping across the East River.

Over the next four months, Washington fought a series of retreats. The British landed halfway up Manhattan Island, trying to surround the American forces again. Washington abandoned New York City and moved north to Harlem Heights, where his troops temporarily stopped the British advance. Then the Americans moved again, this time to White Plains, New York. Finally, the Continental Army was forced to retreat across New Jersey, with General Cornwallis and his Redcoats in hot pursuit.

The long battle was a disaster for the Patriots, with thousands of men killed, wounded, or captured. New York City was lost to the British, who now secured the city as a base.

On September 22, 1776, captured Connecticut Ranger Captain Nathan Hale was executed as a spy by the British. Before his hanging, he uttered the words that captured the Patriot spirit of determination: "I only regret that I have but one life to give for my country." Hale was just 21 years old.

The situation was bleak for the Americans. With Washington and the remnants of his army on the run, the entire war seemed over. The British were convinced they had put down the rebellion. In his pamphlet *The American Crisis*, Thomas Paine wrote, "These are the times that try men's souls." But wily George Washington had a few tricks left up his sleeve. Most of all, the fighting spirit of the Americans endured.

TIMELINE

APRIL 19, 1775
The Battles of Lexington and Concord are fought in Massachusetts, west of Boston. The fighting marks the beginning of the American Revolution.

MAY 10, 1775
The Second Continental Congress convenes in Philadelphia, Pennsylvania.

MAY 10, 1775
British-held Fort Ticonderoga in northeastern New York is captured by American forces led by Ethan Allen and Benedict Arnold.

JUNE 14, 1775
The Second Continental Congress officially creates the Continental Army.

JUNE 15, 1775
George Washington is named commander of the Continental Army.

JUNE 17, 1775
The Battle of Bunker (Breed's) Hill during the siege of Boston, Massachusetts.

JULY 3, 1775
General George Washington arrives in Boston, Massachusetts, to take command of American forces.

DECEMBER 31, 1775
American invasion of Canada halted after defeat at the Battle of Québec.

FEBRUARY 27, 1776
American loyalists are defeated at the Battle of Moore's Creek Bridge, North Carolina.

MARCH 17, 1776
British forces evacuate Boston, Massachusetts, sailing to a temporary base in Halifax, Nova Scotia.

JUNE 28, 1776
British invasion fleet defeated at the Battle of Fort Sullivan, South Carolina.

JULY 4, 1776
Declaration of Independence signed.

AUGUST 27-29, 1776
George Washington's forces defeated at the Battle of Long Island, New York.

A war drum with the painted state seal of Massachusetts.

GLOSSARY

COLONY

A group of people who settle in a distant territory but remain citizens of their native country.

FLANKING MANEUVER

A military term that describes attacking one or both sides of an enemy force. A successful flanking maneuver partially surrounds the enemy and limits maneuverability. It is also a severe psychological shock to enemy forces to be flanked. Panic often results, causing the enemy to flee the battlefield.

FRENCH AND INDIAN WAR

A war fought between 1754-1763 in North America between the forces of France and Great Britain and the two countries's Native American allies. It was part of a larger worldwide conflict called the Seven Years' War.

HESSIANS

Troops from several regions of today's Germany were often paid mercenaries who fought for the British military. They came from places such as Bavaria, Brunswick, Anhalt, Hesse-Cassel, and Hesse-Hanau. The two Hesse realms provided the most troops, so Americans referred to any German soldier as a "Hessian." About 30,000 Hessians served in North America during the American Revolution. They had a reputation, even among the British, as being skilled and ruthless in battle. Thousands of Hessians, however, deserted and fought for the Americans. There were also many Americans of German decent who fought in the war.

MILITIA

Citizens who were part-time soldiers rather than professional army fighters. Militiamen, such as the Minutemen from Massachusetts, usually fought only in their local areas and continued with their normal jobs when they were not needed.

MUSKET

A single-shot weapon, fired from the shoulder, that resembles a modern rifle. Muskets have smooth bores (the inside of the barrel). Their accuracy and range were limited, but a volley of muskets from a large group of soldiers could be quite deadly.

PARLIAMENT

The law-making body of Great Britain. It consists of the House of Lords and the House of Commons.

PATRIOTS

Colonists who rebelled against Great Britain during the American Revolution.

REDOUBT

A fort, or system of trenches and raised earthen berms. Redoubts are used to protect troops against frontal attacks. During the American Revolution they were temporary defensive structures often constructed of logs, piled dirt, or stones and bricks.

TORIES

American colonists who supported Great Britain during the American Revolution. Also called "loyalists."

INDEX